Flareup of Twosomes

FLAREUP
of twosomes

· ·

POEMS *by* Bill Pearlman

LINOCUTS *by* Jim Jacob

La Alameda Press :: New Mexico

Grateful acknowledgement for encouraging
the process of this book emerging:
Neil Nelson, Larry Goodell, Peter Marin, Rebecca Peterson,
Charles Whitt, Gus Blaisdell, David Abel and,
especially, Jeff Bryan who worked with me
all the way to help shape the book.

ISBN: 0-9631909-9-7
Library of Congress Number: 96-84340

La Alameda Press
9636 Guadalupe Trail NW
Albuquerque, New Mexico 87114

But we will learn to submit
each of us to the balanced eternal orbit
wherein we circle our fate
in strange conjunction.

D.H. Lawrence

BRIGHT FLARES *of* LONGING

"Everything that suddenly lights up, draws our joy, flares with beauty—each bush a God burning: this is the alchemical sulphur, the flammable face of the world, its aureole of desire, enthymesis everywhere. That fat of goodness we reach toward as consumers is the active image in each thing, the active imagination of the anima mundi that fires the heart and provokes it out."
JAMES HILLMAN • *Thought of the Heart*

These poems search out the rise and fall of those bright flares of longing that drive us toward each other. In another sense, a mining goes on here that reflects the contradictory power of romantic entanglement. There is an old myth still enthralling the American psyche that says (as if in a dream) we can reach pinnacles of beauty and power second to none. The takeoff is of such tremendous urge to splendor that the grounding is seldom of a piece with the original intention. That initial recurring thrill of bodies comes to a rumour of perfection—it will take you to the main event when the eventualities of loss and sorrow stumble into view.

Heartfelt inevitability enters new zones of heaven and earth. What is the heart? Where does it live and how do we keep it aglow—where there is shadow and doubt and all these lost loves? The heart moves toward the deeps. Nourished by imagination, the heart is swept into the alchemical fire where satisfactions of light transform endlessly.

Spoiling for the sacred, we try to give it a home. Written efforts comes to the fore and ask to be heard. They are of a piece with the urge to song, a fullness in the living sphere. Various intensities of this cohering fire mediate in language and keep us company. And, sometimes, in a combustion of numinous enchantment, real elemental desire enters the chamber, sparking an earnest marriage of opposites—the alert timing that makes way for a soul to be born in the world.

B.P.
Placitas, New Mexico

*for the animated
Ones*

Outside time
looks spacious in here
rooms adjusted to light.
Look in the paper
and big deals all around
films with wrap-around sound
What would you do to be...?
And just so often it leaks
from an elaborate sky
a premise to continue—
forming phrases
kicking the jambs free
wilding the motionless air.
You are here for just this:
pounding out a living
ripping a shot to the corner
where nothing can be found
where a heart spins on a table.

Spoken an undying source—
it lives on its own
it runs where no one knows
it gives power in the mind
it stays determined.
We grow out past
the neverending force
and, driven by invisible powers
it settles in gathered flame.

What grows on between
the two horns
of the old dilemma,
running now
as the heart learns another dance
makes us pour a solid desire
back to square one.

One another aspiring
and all in time.
In one way or another,
a heart to keep us going.
The long walks, the surges,
the jungle in
the dark dream.
What are you doing here?
And what begins growing here
where there is rarity and slumber
and a ghost of a chance.

Gut the shambles perforce
and get used to ambivalence.
Marks the double feel
you've had all along
the male and the female
the yin and the yang
crosscoloring a minus one
and getting clear on the coast—
a swelling of wave and wind.

But who is doing this to us?
a damn riddle, two realms
split and passing,
able to put us right
if only we cleanse the mirror
finally
put ourselves in the other
perhaps darker realm all along?

I call us out
in the sun.
Blocking the keen mystery,
a cloud, a bruise
in the very issue of time,
this study in doubt and shame.
You drink when all's decline
and the taste is right.
Sorrow comes in its own way,
plummets to the edge
where there is recovery
or doom.

Maybe love not so
foresee-able.
The prong
dangling in the sea,
the hook in the mouth.
You get used to it,
this sudden eclipse
of light-giving ports.
I'm the one in the angle,
making way, jousting,
coming into the open.

How else you trot out
the old profusion
scolds a darkness,
all this looking opens me,
see you behind everything,
latin and spark and a swift
image past all remonstrance.

The beast shines
in the whole intrusion,
makes its way,
shapes an innermost cause,
pushes the leads in
makes what matters
rise in the flesh.

Along the sudden way,
a whole flareup of twosomes,
goes through the bin,
and you bounce back,
coaxes such ingenious
leads past all the dark
opens you this
fashionable twist, this floorshow.

You read back to me
and it hit home.
The sound filled the room
with feminine power
and I was simply there,
listening to your voice,
my words
the inclusive
harmony of shared vocation
into the soil of our depth
into the reach of our cries.

Flesh enlivens the tired daze.
You want a place for your horns.
Feels good,
drives deep
removes a fade and cry.
I'm not sure what to say.
Get ready
for unpeeling,
a robe
round a central post.

The close calls, the perils,
the dream disorders.
One stays,
another falls in line.
You know how to help some,
others go to the edge,
gets crowded
so much of the scene.
Corn is applauded,
gold rises occasionally.
I wanted darkest mystery
unfolded light in the background.
But it was never to be,
stood its part only for a glimpse.

How you stood
in the infinity of song!
How the world worked
its way into the mood
where the sharp-tongued fires
supported the reels of vision.
I want you
to enjoin me, to stand
the intermittent force
staged beckoned and farewelled.

Open wide.
Get back to what's spoken—
your life, means
and your nexus:

What do you do?
What calls you into play?
What plan works?

and what the hell
collides with the day
ruins what peace there is?

Never enough pure direction
caught in orbit a thing
mindlessly moves
we climb old stairs
bags in hand,
unknown clerks ask our cause
seek our entry fees.
Our flag flies on the ship
we have just arrived.
Good you know our tongue
we will need food and quarter.

Half-dead horse
fathomless.
You bought a lousy fake.
It don't talk.
It don't add strength.
You cain't ride it.

Here and there.
How do I announce the morning?
Another surety, a bond
with what life brings.
Cannot halt the process—
leaps incessantly
everything
in the heart sweeps us
into innocence and a field
we almost see through.
We haunt a foretold pleasure to be here,
juicing the veins past the rinds,
put lips to joy, smacking
while all kinds of demise abounds.
What will you give me for a look
past curt irregular findings,
at the edge of forgiveness,
dense forest where we retrieve
fierce allegiance.

No need to say a word
calamity the engine
downsizing
of all proportion,
the decline of what looked
like flourishing
for an instant.

But I live here
my own world-sphere
my legs
heart lips mine
shareable sure
but madness overtakes
vigilance
and I don't need it
can't take it
so go
I'll go.

What if it's been centuries
this space filled with human
longing
for warmth (how many times?)
swell with tense pride.
Wrapped in flesh
utterly
soft the turning toward one
who wills the sun brightening
the cliffs clear roughness
my mind sails a hawk searching
staring idly into a great distance.

Back to the garden
source and soil edge of one's life,
pull the seeds in and up
perfect suspension
she believes in what comes
the best row of tomato plants
just little beginnings
who knows the body
the way we use ground
for what the sun inspires
in late March
the fullness mysterium
replanted only to be reborn
the secret
never lost, the shrewd plants
how likely to join four basics
in a thrust never to be outdone
climb invisible channels
seeds resurrect lovelust
a point we can share.

What best intended
a form of rising
you grew toward
you kept singing
just so
slip or live
from urge to urge
part to part.

I needed to leave
head out where
there was bravery & fullness
where I might make a creation
or put brain into focus
dance where you put the ripest wish
in the diametry of forgiveness
there was betrayal of trust
kinship with so many leavings

so much we want startles us
tools that send us into overdrive
to feel alert and present
to make a decision or keep a date
but still old chaos
the rising and falling modes
stretch us
toward the veritable summit
shine like the presence of the almighty
in fluid exchange with eternity.

Can't go on   go on
some thing happens no thing
bright incursion along dark
trail that leads nowhere
miles along the beach
fresh sand
feet plod away up there hills
bet a beer would taste good
wait for the right question
isn't this extraordinary health
in the beamwork, bright sky
stars later
what can I do will
make this hardness melt?

Coax the infinite back again
and start to grieve
you missed something
whatever the time
that scrawls the plenitude
back again. I want to fulfill
all that privilege imploded in me,
what the sanctuary founded
within this turning world
and the exact proportions of what
may be implanted
in the heart
drives its interior forward
dawning in the momentum
amazes a certainty
that knows no boundary
a pledge that this life
consists in finding
the pure exemplary cohesion.

What once stood here within
brings rumors of steady power
an overwhelming need
to score the rapture
would enclose all we crave
bright beckoning
in so many halls
great leaps will not quite rise
only the deepened dream sense
of disconnect
does not belong in all its forms
comes from so much that races

a slow form which doesn't
glue to easy fabric

but lunges out where
steady gain
still in the open.

Hoist what you bring
into its own
give us this day our bread
that rears toward
fidelity to onward
you will get up to the mark soon

you will drive apace a rare breed
nod in the right direction
make way
where fluent actions awake
what we crave
a future
that makes true
the invalidating curve
the nexus
that startles the alive
to bargain again.

Be kind in the meantime
it all hooks
into future whirl
I love the namesakes
of all that we do
the pride that rides
where we bless
& tread the old highway.

It manages me an old opposition
knowing how long I can be here
how true to my mission I gaze
across all the obstacles, the briefings
times left me homeless
run up the tab on hope, drop
a few names as outcalls
mobbed in pandemonium
cornered the blue corn
staggered the imaginal.

So sweetly we enjoin
in growing abundance
all looks out over world shadows
& makes way down new roads.

What brightens
is love that awakens thought
courage and the future
overloading the ripest curve
the shapeliest doubt
that tunnels into the heart.

Heave-ho and all the fire
extends to rich bodily living,
a strange majesty overwhelms
we drive into colorful riddles
settle old disputes
arrange our subtle fire inward
shape the lowliest senses
broad range of altitudes & mesas.

All through this exempt
condition that wanders far & wide
in the name of contingency
or the awake members of the tribe

you used to be great
the times you passed through the membranes
of every member notwithstanding
goes to the heart of matter

what we do is crawl toward destiny
no ceremony to antidote
what's been done to us—

we fight one & all
a delight in the making free
ask what you may find
in the momentary
divulgence.

Just as well we make it flare
in each body, a schedule
unflappingly conjoins
with magnificent particulars
of joust & dance,
reverberate the night sky
one more adjustment
rares its moorings
as what we want
scrambles inward
and nobody even names
the ingredients now.

We come as best we can
and there is a sudden
blackout or swollen
lead that catches us
in the unbalance.
Sift through worlds
put the heart into
the vast hidden,
the precise periodicity
that gleams here.

Heartily again, the sweet
enjoyment, the calculable
flood, that enters us,
comes as it may toward the wind
howls and befuddles all
while surely a current
runs in the veins,
a window opening
on the unbreached distance.

I want simply to incandesce
or remove myself
in the crevice
that stands its own embodiment,
that pushes us to the test
of all we inherit.
I employ the true shift—
the wayward sense we all share
we want to shine like a great star.

Sturdy calling
now & then
bright purpose along roads
keep travelling along ridden highs
you get there now & then
I'm ok all through the vineyards
bright bunched in the daylight
way out of bounds
it cools me
out in the sun, great job all told
light & voids all thrusting
tears in the meantime, yes
I could shape you, could
bring you into my own, right

through to the entity forgives the insider's pledge.

I wanted all there was
and settled for less
though figuring
that doubted was a redoubled paradox
and the lilt was fabulous
just over the Bridge
where it all hung out
while we hungered
for a view
collided with eternity.

Just once will you please
hark back to a destiny
manage feverish touch
wild thread
that romanced the yeast
will make us all rise.

But your youth vanishes
no fame catches up to it
& the body furnishes rooms
of boredom.

Get me off
this heavy planet
once in awhile fervent
sliding the trombone into the zone
frying a waffle in the backyard.

This is the room where light
shines evanescent brooding
toward magnificence.

These referentials along the way
& out in the frontierland
a shoulder to lean on.

What became of Sweet Sue
or the outcrop of lovely faces
that gathered near the river.

I know how long it takes
for us to drive inward
running up the tab on joy

range the peaks the dance
put us firmly in the wake
or darling flush of chance.

All implodes & darkly
round
the old pivot
a dance
that matters
sends us deeper
storm in the meantime
where need & recess
a way to skip through the light
bound toward the ruins

take us toward the transformer.

Conclusive?
it heads out
into the brave west

comes down the pike
to learn the figures of the dawn

bunches at the pass
& the sweet formulations

that gather the seed in the body
put it close to the head

fills with rapture
closes the burnt offering.

Back on himself again
strumming the hymnal
going to such ends

long last it includes merriment
almost ready to perform
and leap into the heartfelt
ending that aspires to beginning.

Put the *we* back in and storm
the eclectic harmonic. We need
the way we once turned
to the other,
shaping a fierce overlay,
a bedrock loveliness we extend
to the many who come our way.

COLOPHON

Set in *Goudy Modern*.
Designed by Frederic Goudy in *1918*,
this face has deep color
carried in curves
whose syncopation
enlivens white space.
Mr. Goudy was originally inspired
by a caption beneath a
French engraving
of a scene from Ovid.

Book design by J. Bryan

Bill Pearlman, actor, playwright, therapist,
lives in Placitas, New Mexico.
His previous books include:
Surfing Off the Ark;
Elegy for Prefontaine;
Inzorbital: A Novel; and
Characters of the Sacred:
The World of Archetypal Drama

•

Residing in Albuquerque, Jim Jacob is
a painter and printmaker widely known
for his explorations of iconography.